Jiriki ↔ tariki   opposites

Suzuki + Zen no dualism — union of opposites

SHIN
BUDDHISM

SHIN BUDDHISM

HARPER & ROW, PUBLISHERS
New York, Evanston, and London

D. T. Suzuki

SHIN BUDDHISM. Copyright © 1970 by American Buddhist Academy. All rights reserved. Printed in the United States of America. No part of this book may be used or reproduced in any manner whatsoever without written permission except in the case of brief quotations embodied in critical articles and reviews. For information address Harper & Row, Publishers, Inc., 49 East 33rd Street, New York, N.Y. 10016. Published simultaneously in Canada by Fitzhenry & Whiteside Limited, Toronto.

FIRST EDITION

LIBRARY OF CONGRESS CATALOG CARD NUMBER: 71-86908

CONTENTS

	PREFACE	9
ONE	Love and Compassion As Infinite Light	13
TWO	The Enlightenment of the Inner Self	25
THREE	The Reality of Faith	43
FOUR	The Futility of Pride	57
FIVE	The Excellence of man	75
	About the Author	93

SHIN BUDDHISM

PREFACE

Where did I come from into this world?
Where am I going after death?

I came alone into this world and am departing alone to the next world. If there were no compassion toward me from the other-power, my past, present, and future would not exist. To protect, and to guide me, there are countless powers. For example—my parents, my society, my nation, the air, earth, sun, etc.—all these pow-

PREFACE

ers of compassion are called Oyasama. I cannot live in this world without Oyasama. Oyasama and I are in Oneness. Oyasama is the infinite light and life that is called Amida Buddha.

In Japanese, *Namu* means myself. *Namu Amida Butsu* is an expression of oneness—in other words, Oyasama and I. Therefore when we recite *Namu Amida Butsu* it is an expression of gratitude for this universal compassion which is always within us and surrounding us, regardless of whether we recognize or accept it.

We came into this world with Oyasama and will return to Oyasama after our death. Oyasama is the source of joy, hope, and gratefulnesss.

Dr. Daisetsu Suzuki, the world-renowned Buddhist scholar, presented a series of lectures on Oyasama, a Japanese expression of great compassion which is also the Shinshu teaching, the truth of naturalness. The five lectures were sponsored by the American Buddhist Academy and taped in the spring of 1958 at the main hall of the New York Buddhist Church.

My dear friends Mr. and Mrs. Robert Blickenderfer, who had never met Dr. Suzuki or heard his lectures, were anxious to hear the tapes—they were greatly impressed and decided to transcribe the taped lectures for publication, in order that others too may enjoy the immensity of Dr. Suzuki's knowledge and wisdom on Buddism.

Their great effort and patience have made this publication possible, for which I am deeply grateful.

THE REVEREND HOZEN SEKI
President, American Buddhist Academy

one

LOVE AND COMPASSION AS INFINITE LIGHT

The Pure Land school of teaching was originated in China, but it accomplished its full development in the Shin school of Pure Land teaching. The Shin school is the culmination of Pure Land thought, and that took place in Japan. The Japanese may not have offered very many original ideas to world thought or world culture, but in Shin we find a major contribution the Japanese can make to the outside world and all the other Buddhist schools. There is one other Buddhist school that developed in Japan—Nichiren. But all the other schools more or less trace their origin as well as their form either to China or to India. Nichiren is somewhat related to the nationalistic spirit of Japan and is often confused with nationalism. But Shin is absobutely free from such connections. In that respect, Shin is remarkable.

Shinran (1173-1262), the founder of the Shin sect, lived in Kyoto, Japan. He is generally said to be of noble lineage, but that, I suspect, is fiction. He must have been more than just an ordinary man, and probably he belonged to a relatively cultured family, but he did not belong to the nobility. He might have had some connection with a noble family in Japan, but his training, his real religious development, took place when he was exiled to the country, far away from the capital, the center of culture in Japan in those days. He was a follower of Honen, founder of the Pure Land doctrine in Japan. Honen's influence was extensive at the time. Old priests, belonging to the traditional school, were not pleased with Honen's popularity, and somehow they contrived to have him banished into the country.

Shinran, was also exiled to the northern part of Japan, and his actual religious experience took place while he was in the country, living among rural people. Shinran had a profound understanding of the needs of the common people. In those days Buddhism was a somewhat aristocratic religion; the study of Buddhism was mainly confined to the learned people, who were rather addicted to education. But Shinran knew that education was not the way to reach religious experience. There had to be a more direct way, a religious experience that did not require any medium of learning or ritualism. All such things had to be cast aside in order for one to have religious experience, to have the full awakening of the religious consciousness. Shinran experienced this himself, and he finally found the most direct way to the experience.

Of all the development Mahayana Buddhism has achieved in the Far East, the most remarkable one is the Shin teaching of the Pure Land school. It is remarkable chiefly because geographically its birthplace is Japan and historically it is the latest evolution of Pure Land Mahayana, and therefore the highest point it has reached. The Pure Land idea grew first in India. Sutras used by that sect were compiled in India, so ideas must have developed there, and the sutras devoted to its exposition were compiled probably about three hundred years after Buddha, that is, about one or two centuries before the Christian era. The Pure Land school started in India toward the end of the fifth century, when the White Lotus Society was organized by Huineng or *Eon* in Japanese and his friends in 403 A.D. The idea of a Buddha Land, presided over by Buddha, is as old as Buddhism, but the school based on the desire to be born in such a land, in order to attain the final end of the Buddhist life, did not fully materialize until Buddhism began to flourish in China as a practical religion. It took the Japanese genius of the thirteenth century to mature it further into the teaching of the Shin school.

Pure Land doctrine is ordinarily quite heavy-laden with all kinds of what I term accretions. These technicalities and appendages are not necessary for modern people to comprehend in order to get at the gist of the doctrine.

For instance, Amida is the focus of the Pure Land doctrine. He is represented as being so many feet tall and endowed with all the admirable physical qualities of a great man; he emits light beams from his body, illuminating all the worlds—the entire universe, not just one world—so many worlds that they defy our human calculation of measurement; every ray of light that comes out of his body, from every pore of his skin, is many Buddhas, and is thus decorated in a most extravagant way, beyond human imagination.

Of course this view is the product of human imagination, so I can't say it is beyond human imagination.

Love and Compassion as Infinite Light

But Indian minds are richly endowed with the ability to create imagery. Indians are the only people so extraordinarily gifted in that faculty. When you read the sutras and listen to the old way of explaining Pure Land doctrine, you are staggered at the disparity between the Indian interpretation and the modern way of thinking and viewing such things. I am not going to go into the embroidered orthodox doctrine, so my explanation may seem somewhat prosaic and devoid of the glamor and rich imagery of the traditional Indian view.

In a way, Amida has been brought down to the earth; however, the doctrine is not to be treated from the intellectual point of view or on our relative, earthly plane of thought. It is altogether beyond human intellection, but at the same time, Pure Land and Amida are revealed on this earth, although not as taught by orthodox preachers. Pure Land is not many millions of millions of miles away in the West. According to my explanation, Pure Land is right here, and those who have eyes can see it around them. And Amida is not presiding over an ethereal paradise, but his Pure Land is this dirty earth itself. It is now apparent that my Pure Land doctrine will go directly against the traditional or conventional explanation. But I have my own explanation, and perhaps my interpretation will lead you to agree with my views.

A friend in Brazil recently wrote to me, requesting

that I write out essential teachings of the Pure Land sect in English, because it is difficult to translate Japanese into Portuguese. He wanted me also to present the doctrine in such a manner that it would emphasize its similarity to Christian theology, to show Amida and Pure Land doctrine at least superficially close to Christianity and yet to retain characteristic features of the doctrine. So I sent an explanation to him. Whether he agreed with it or not, I do not know. At any rate I kept a copy for my own "edification," and I shall share parts of it with you.

I said: We believe in Amida Butsu, Amida Buddha, as Savior of all beings. "Savior" is not a word that is frequently used among Buddhists; it is rather a kind of condescension to the Christian phraseology. Amida Buddha is eternal life and infinite light. All beings are born in sin and burdened with sin. Of course, the idea of sin must be specially interpreted to give it Buddhist color.

Second, we believe in Amida Buddha as our Oyasama or Oyasan, as it is sometimes called. *San* is occasionally used rather than *sama*, but Oyasama is the usual term. Oyasama means, in this context, love and compassion. Strictly speaking, there is no word corresponding to Oyasama in English or any European languages. *Oya* means parent, but not both parents, since *sama*, as used

Love and Compassion as Infinite Light

here, is an honorific. Thus *Oya* means not either of the parents, but both mother and father; not separate personalities, but both fatherly qualities and mother qualities united in one personality. In Christianity God is addressed as Father: "Our Father which art in heaven," but Oyasama is not in heaven, nor is Oyasama the Father. It is incorrect to say "he" or "she," for no sexuality is involved. I don't like to say "it," so I don't know what to say. Oyasama is a unique word, deeply endearing and at the same time rich with religious significance.

Third, we believe that salvation—"salvation" is not a good term here, but I am trying to comply with my friend's request—consists in pronouncing the name of Amida in sincerity and devotion. Pronouncing the name of Amida may not be considered very important, but a name has certain magical powers and when a name is uttered, the object bearing that name appears before one. In *The Arabian Nights*, when the devil's name is pronounced, the devil appears. And among primitive people the name of a god or supreme being is sacred, revealed only to those initiates who have participated in certain rituals. The initiate is led by the eldest leader of the religion into a dense forest, where there is no danger of being overheard by anybody. Then the elder tells God's name to the initiate. By knowing the name, the initiate is now fully qualified as a leader. A name is highly significant in religious life. Amida's name is pronounced in sincerity and with devotion. The formula is *Namu Amida Butsu*. Butsu is Buddha. *Namu* means "I take refuge." I take refuge in Amida Buddha. Or we may take Namu as meaning adoration to Buddha. It is a simple formula. There is nothing mysterious about it, and you may wonder how such a name, or such a phrase, could have a wonderful power for all beings. But love is experienced by all beings when *Namu Amida Butsu* is pronounced with single-mindedness.

I might also mention *hongan*. Hongan, according to my interpretation, is the primal will, and this primal will is at the foundation of all reality. *Hongan* as expressed in the Amida sutra—there are forty-eight, but forty-eight may be all summarized in one *hongan*, which is: *Amida wants to save all beings*. Amida desires that all beings be brought over to his land, the land of purity and bliss. And those who earnestly, sincerely, devotedly believe in Amida will all be born in the Pure Land. This birth does not take place after what is called death. Instead of being born in the Pure Land, for sincere followers, Pure Land itself is created; it comes into existence when we sincerely pronounce *Namu Amida Butsu*. Therefore, instead of our going over to the Pure Land, it comes to us. In a way, we are carry-

Love and Compassion as Infinite Light

ing the Pure Land all along, and when we pronounce that magic formula *Namu Amida Butsu,* we become conscious of the presence of the Pure Land around us, or in us.

I have to explain *hongan* further, I think. *Hon* means original, or primal. And *gan* is generally translated "vow," although that may not be an adequate equivalent. Sometimes it is translated "prayer," "wish," or "desire." More philosophically, it may be better to say "will," as in "primal will." Why *gan* is not properly to be translated "vow" or "prayer," "wish" or "desire," will become clearer later.

Some may wonder how the Mahayana could have expanded itself into the doctrine of Pure Land, which apparently stands in direct contrast to the Buddha's supposedly original teachings of self-reliance and enlightenment by means of *prajna*.

Amida stands on one side, and on the other side stands *bombu*—just ordinary people, as we all are. Furthermore, Amida is *hō*, in contrast to *ki*. *Hō* and *ki* are very difficult terms to translate. *Hō* is on the other side and *ki* is on this side, and religious teachings start from the relationship between *hō* and *ki*. *Hō* might be considered as corresponding to God or Christ, and *ki* is the sinful personality. In *hō* we have other-power, and *ki* is self-power. Other-power and self-power stand in contrast, and to be born in the Pure Land, one must altogether abandon self-power and embrace the other-power. In fact, when other-power is embraced by self-power, self-power turns into other-power, or other-power takes up self-power altogether. On one side we have Pure Land, and on the other side this world. This world is commonly called, in Japanese and Chinese—really it is a Sanskrit term originally—*shaba*. The other world is *jodo*. *Jo* is "Pure," *do* means "Land"—*jodo*, Pure Land. *Shaba* is, we might say, the land of defilement, defiled land, and in contrast is the land of purity, Pure Land. Pure Land is the realm of the absolute, and *shaba* is the realm of relativity. Perhaps this will be enough to explain.

When we say *Namu Amida Butsu*, *Namu* represents self-power—*ki*. *Amida* is *hō*, the other-power. *Namu Amida Butsu* symbolizes the unification of *ki* and *hō*, Amida and *bompu*, self-power and other-power, and *shaba*, Pure Land, and this world, unified, identified. So when *Namu Amida Butsu* is pronounced, it represents, or symbolizes, a unification of the two. Unification is not an adequate term, but its meaning will become clear.

Now Amida is on the other side and the *bompu* on this side and *shaba* where we are. Pure Land reveals itself when we realize what we are, or rather what Amida is. Other-power is very much emphasized in Shin teaching. When Amida and other-power are understood, Pure Land will inevitably become significant too. When Amida's essential quality is comprehended, *hongan* and compassion, or love, will also accompany Amida. It is like just holding the central part. If you pull the middle up, all the rest comes with it.

two

THE ENLIGHTENMENT OF THE INNER SELF

Amida Buddha was once a human being, but it is rather difficult to determine exactly how long ago he lived. It was a long, long time ago, and when he was a human being he was one of the sons of a great king. When he saw how miserable human life was, he wanted to extricate people from such a wretched existence and bring them onto the other shore of the stream of birth and death. He was so compassionate that he felt all the sufferings of other people as if they were his own. His interest in all beings was unstained by selfishness. It was altogether altruistic. Ordinarily, whatever interest we may take in others is grounded in self-interest. Some people go so far as to say that we are devoid of altruistic impulse, but I cannot agree with such views. We have altruistic impulses, and we often show evidence that we do. We forget ourselves and risk our lives for others, and in pursuing that course of conduct we don't think about anything. We do it impulsively, indicating our actions arise from our ignorant nature.

The Amida Buddha generally is shown to represent this altruistic impulse that is deeply rooted in human nature, perhaps rooted in the cosmos itself. To achieve altruism, according to the Indian way of thinking, one must be pure of all defiled sentiment or feelings or emotions; otherwise he cannot expect to save others. So the Amida Buddha wanted to perfect himself.

Another doctrine generally held by Indian thinkers or religious leaders is that when one attains spiritual perfection, the place where he is situated, or his environment, changes with him. That is, when a person attains enlightenment—moral perfection—the environment in which he finds himself also changes according to his

The Enlightenment of the Inner Self

subjectivity. When Amida attained enlightenment, therefore, his environment changed in the same way he himself did. The country or realm, wherever he was, changed with him and became a place conducive for other people to attain enlightenment. Other people who come to that country, which is called the Pure Land, will attain enlightenment without struggling against odds or against undesirable circumstances.

When he was living as a human being, there was a great Buddha from whom Amida wanted to receive enlightenment to make himself fit for the creation of a Pure Land. This Buddha made Amida see all the lands of which he could make a choice, and Amida chose the Pure Land. Some lands were not absolutely pure, some were mixed with purities and defilements, and others were not altogether desirable, so he chose the Pure Land, where there was no stain of defilement or impurities.

Amida disciplined himself for many years, or many *kalpas*, you might say—in the Indian tradition a *kalpa* is an extremely long period; in fact, it goes almost beyond human calculation. With patience enough, mathematicians might determine it, or modern machines might compute it, but for ordinary people like ourselves it is beyond our calculation. And Amida trained himself morally; that is, he practiced what are known as the six virtues of perfection. He went through that discipline for many *kalpas*, and many more *kalpas*, and he finally attained enlightenment.

But before he attained enlightenment (along with enlightenment Pure Land also comes to exist), he made a vow. In fact, he made forty-eight vows, but one of the vows, which is favored by the Shin people, is most important, and without that vow other vows lose their miraculous powers of helping beings. The important vow is the eighteenth. It is mentioned in the larger sutra of eternal life. That vow translated from Chinese reads something like: "If, upon my obtaining Buddhahood, that is, obtaining enlightenment, all beings in the Ten Quarters should not desire in sincerity and trustfulness to be born in my country, and if they should not be born there by only thinking of me for, say, up to ten times—except those who have committed the five grave offenses and those who are abusive of the true Dharma—may I not obtain the highest enlghtenment."

Now in this vow it is most important to have the desire to be born in Amida's country, not just superficially or lightheartedly, but in sincerity, in earnestness, most seriously and trusting fully in Amida's power to make us born there. At the same time one must pronounce his name, *Namu Amida Butsu*. According to Shin, just one time is enough, but this sutra says "up to

The Enlightenment of the Inner Self

ten times." In fact, just once pronouncing Amida's name is enough, but if once is enough, then ten times will also be enough. We might repeat his name many times, ever so many times, but we must pronounce the name in sincerity, really desiring to be born in his country—to be born in his country means to obtain enlightenment as Amida by himself did. We cannot just desire to be born into the Pure Land, but the object of being born there is to attain enlightenment.

This *shaba* world, this world of relativity, is not conducive to our attainment of perfect enlightenment. But here the theory of environment is particularly valid. Environment is a large factor in shaping our personality, but at the same time our personality has a great effect on our environment, too. So environment and the persons living in it—all Buddhisms and the environment in which they live—are mutually reactive.

Anyway, we sincerely pronounce the Amida's vows, fully trusting that they will work out. To utter the name once with trustfulness and sincerity is enough, but generally we do not pronounce it sincerely. We may think we are sincere and in possession of full faith or belief in Amida or somebody else, but real faith, real sincerity, is altogether devoid of such consciousness. As long as sincerity is conscious of itself, it is not genuine. So sincerity does not say, "I am sincere."

Such an attitude may remain just a little bit, even unnoticeably or insignificantly, in the depth of the unconscious, and although unconsciousness cannot be consciousness, still something of consciousness is submerged there. And because that consciousness is left in the unconscious, it comes up sometimes unexpectedly and says: Why, I am so sincere, and yet people don't believe me! When we feel this way, even when we are most sincere we are not sincere at all.

When we pronounce Amida's name while such consciousness remains, we cannot be born in the Pure Land. Therefore, to pronounce *Namu Amida Butsu* is to forget altogether, is to be not conscious of saying *Namu Amida Butsu*. But when I identify myself with *Namu Amida Butsu* and forget that I am the person who is pronouncing that name, or that *myōgō*, it is still not enough. Even when I feel that the *myōgō* itself, the name itself, is pronouncing itself, that *Namu Amida Butsu* is pronouncing itself, still that is not sincerity if consciousness is left.

Sincerity is perfectly forgetting one's self, but at the same time not just forgetting. In an ordinary way we forget many things and do all kinds of things, but not that kind of forgetfulness. Religious or spiritual forgetfulness, spiritually turning into the unconscious, is—well, one has personally to experience what kind of forgetfulness or unconsciousness it is.

The Enlightenment of the Inner Self

Now with this vow we follow his advice, or his instruction, and this sincerity is obtained; then enlightenment becomes a reality. But according to Shin teaching, in this relative existence of ours, however sincere we might try to be, still a certain amount of insincerity is with us. It is inevitable. Relative existence and insincerity are always inextricably interrelated. The final conclusion is that as long as we live in this world, attainment of perfect enlightenment is impossible. So if we go to the Pure Land where no stain of relativity—it is known as defilement—no such remnant or residue of relativity is left, then that is the most fit place for enlightenment to take place. Amida vowed this.

Finally, after disciplining himself for many *kalpas*, Amida obtained enlightenment. In another part of the sutra Amida vows, "When I obtain enlightenment and all beings do not obtain enlightenment, may I not attain the highest enlightenment." Therefore his attainment of enlightenment is dependent upon our obtaining of enlightenment. This is quite a difficult concept, and I leave much of it to your own thinking. This may appear to be lazy on my part, but I think it is the best.

Some people say, "Amida obtained enlightenment, and he has his own Pure Land—what is the use of our pronouncing his name and wishing to be born in the Pure Land?" The very fact that Amida obtained his enlightenment shows that we also have already obtained our enlightenment. We received it when Amida attained his so many *kalpas* ago. We can say, "We are Buddhas from the very first, from the beginningless beginning. There is no need of our wishing to be born in the Pure Land or our pronouncing *Namu Amida Butsu*. Everything is done on the part of Amida and we simply live just as we like."

But people who live like that, without having anything in their minds, without anxiety about anything, exist like animals—like dogs or cats. They don't think about Amida, getting enlightenment, or being born in the Pure Land. If we could reduce ourselves into a spiritual, mental, or psychological state of mind like that of dogs or cats, it might be all right. In a way, dogs and cats are very much better than we, although ordinarily we think we are superior to them. Strangely enough, we are not content with the state in which we find ourselves. We are always discontented with our environment, and there is a reason for this. Our existence here on earth is really meant to transcend this situation. If in another world we can discover the meaning of existence, the value of life, the value of living—that is what is most important. If we could find the significance of life, the value of existence, then the end of living would be attained and we would have no more desire.

I have been reading Meister Eckhart recently. He says

The Enlightenment of the Inner Self

somebody asks him, "What is eternal life?" Then Eckhart writes in one of his sermons, "Why not ask eternal life itself, instead of asking me?" If you want to know whether you can realize Buddhahood, you had better ask Buddha himself. That was the way Eckhart answered.

This reminds me of a certain devoted Shin layman in Japan some years ago. Although Shoma was an ignorant day laborer, he had a wonderful understanding of Buddhism. It is marvelous that such an illiterate person can grasp the deepest possible meaning, which even learned, scholarly, acute-minded philosophers cannot grasp, finding it too deep for their understanding. This uneducated person understood Buddhism perfectly, and therefore he was well known among his neighbors. Actually, his "neighborhood" extended to many, many miles away, for numerous people living in faraway districts, hearing of Shoma's devotion and extraordinary understanding, came to inquire of him how to be saved or how to be born in the Pure Land or how to come in contact with Amida.

One day a man began his journey from a distant place to see Shoma. In those days there were no railroads or airplanes, so he had to walk several hundred miles. Finally he reached the place where Shoma lived. He found Shoma busily pounding rice, for he was hired by somebody else as a laborer. In ancient times—not very ancient, for I still remember pounding rice myself—rice had to be refined by pounding it in a big mortar and pestle. It is rather hard work, but Shoma was very busily engaged in it when the weary man finally arrived and asked him, "Pray, pray tell me, how can I be born in the Pure Land? How will Amida be gracious enough to look after me?" Shoma, however, went on pounding rice, without paying any attention whatever. But this man, who had come from such a faraway place, importuned Shoma very earnestly. Still Shoma was obdurate and did not even look at him. Then the people of the house where he was hired to pound the rice had mercy on the pitiful traveler and asked Shoma not to be so impolite, so unconcerned. Still Shoma went on pounding. Then the people of the house asked the man to come in and have a rest and a cup of tea.

After some time the traveler, disappointed and in despair, said sadly, "I came such a long way, but if I am not to be told about Amida and his salvation, I can do nothing but return to my home, my native town." He looked miserable. As he was about to depart, Shoma said, "If you are in such a desperate state of mind, you are altogether wrong in asking me about such things. Why don't you go to Amida Sama himself? He is the one who deals with such things. It's not my business." The traveler left, impressed with this thought.

Voltaire is quoted as saying, "To save people is divine business, the business of God, and we don't have anything to do with it. Leave that to God. We don't have to bother with that kind of thing. We should not interfere with God's business." If Voltaire really did say that, he was a great spiritual man. He was an enlightened man like Shoma. Actually, I do not know whether Voltaire had such an exalted spiritual state of mind. That's another matter. But if we take these words in the attitude of most spiritual people, Voltaire is quite right, just as Shoma was right.

You will find that we do not have anything to do with Amida. Amida is an "extraneous" kind of being who occasionally or sporadically or even erratically comes to us—Christians would say, "by divine grace." Divine grace is such an erratic thing that you cannot depend on its being there all the time. Is Amida a real being? My understanding of this part of Shin doctrine is that this sutra, the larger sutra especially, of eternal life, is related in a mythical way. It has almost nothing to do with so-called history.

I was talking with an American philosopher who visited Japan many, many years ago, Dr. William Pratt. He is now dead. He was a great author and he understood Buddhism very well. Dr. Pratt and I were discussing Christianity's emphasis on historical fact and how Christianity depends on history whereas Buddhism ignored what is known as objective history but depends on legend or some kind of mythology.

We came to this conclusion: Myth and legend and tradition—tradition may not be a good term—and poetical imagination are actually more real than what we call factual history. What we call facts are not really facts, are not really so dependable and objective. Real objectivity is in metaphysical subjectivity, you might say, metaphysical truth or poetic legend or religious myth. So we agreed that the Amida story has more objective and spiritual reality than mere historical truth or fact, and Amida has more metaphysical foundation than objective historical fact. Amida is really ourselves—this is the reason why we can accept the story of Amida so easily and understand the story of Shoma and other such devoted people.

In the story itself is something very deep which directly appeals to our inner mind. We can say there is outer mind and inner mind, or outer soul or inner soul. We generally lean on this outer self or outer mind, not the inner or inmost self. The inmost self lies deeply buried in the unfathomable abyss of our relative consciousness. This self is ordinarily well concealed under

The Enlightenment of the Inner Self

layers of all kinds of things moving on the surface of consciousness. That is what we take generally as the real self, but actually it is not real. The real inner self is hard to awaken. And to awaken that inner self, according to Shin doctrine, one pronounces the name of Amida, that is, *Namu Amida Butsu*. But merely to say *Namu Amida Butsu* will never awaken the inner self. As I have said, *Namu Amida Butsu* is to be pronounced in sincerity with real devotion. And our outer self, which is superficial—working on the surface of our consciousness—this superficiality consists in bifurcation. When we think, *This is my self*, or *This is my inner self*, that self is always divided into two—the self and something which stands against that self. When we become conscious of our selves we always have the one who thinks and the one who is thought—object and subject. Subject and object are always present in our consciousness.

The Dhammapada—one of the earliest texts of Buddhism now in our possession—discusses at great length the destroying of consciousness to get rid of consciousness. When people read a statement like "to destroy consciousness," they assume it means negating existence altogether—that is, committing suicide. This is the gospel of negativity, and Western people often criticize it. The Oriental mind is for this reason accused of being negativistic, always denying. But "to destroy consciousness" in fact means to destroy the superficial, relatively working consciousness, to go beyond bifurcation of subject and object. Subject and object, before they split, emerge from where there is yet no subject or object. This world we naturally see is intellectually reconstructed; it is not the real one. We have re-formed it through our senses and our intellect working at the back of those senses. We reconstruct this world and proceed to believe our fabrication is the real thing.

But to reach the inner self, such superficial relativity must be eradicated. Of course this takes a long time to explain. "To destroy relativity," as Buddhists or other religious people use the phrase, is not to create another relativity but to find relativity itself as undivided into relative terms—which, again, is rather difficult to understand. But the inner self is reached only when this relativity is transcended. When there is no subject, no object, some Buddhists would say, we are in a state like that before we were born into this world. We see things as we did before we entered this earth. But to speak this way we usually have to use language.

Language always works in time; therefore, everything we verbalize is chronologically ordered. So I say, "Before I was born," or, "In the state I was before I came into this earth." All such phrases refer to actions which took place in the past; they are time-conditioned, and

The Enlightenment of the Inner Self

our language itself is hampered with this dualism. So when I speak about transcending this attitude of relativity, what do I mean? We can't think. We can never bring such a thing into our consciousness, it is quite true. Consciousness itself is a time product, and to destroy that time product and yet to reproduce it in time, to destroy consciousness which is in time and yet to have whatever experience we get by doing that, seems contradictory. Such an experience expresses itself through consciousness, in consciousness—*in terms of time.* That which goes beyond time we try to express in time. This is a contradiction as long as we appeal to language, but we have no alternative but to appeal to language. So we are in a constant dilemma. But we have to live with that somehow.

And then we know that our real inmost self is where subject and object have not made their appearance. It is as if the world had not yet come into existence. You may ask: What was there before the world came into existence? Such a question simply reveals thought patterns conditioned by time. My answer to it is that before the world came into existence is this present moment, this absolute moment. Metaphysically speaking, such a moment is the time we really experience sincerity, the time we experience what Christians would call "forsaking self." Forsaking self is forsaking relativity of self and getting into the inmost self which knows no subject, no object, no sincerity, no insincerity. When we are conscious of sincerity we are generally also conscious of insincerity, for they are mixed up with each other. When insincerity and sincerity are transcended, then Amida comes into our inner self and identifies himself with this self, or this self finds itself in Amida. And when we find this self in Amida, we are in the Pure Land.

As I said before, we don't go out of this world in order to be born in the Pure Land, but we carry the Pure Land all the time. Being born in the Pure Land means discovering the Pure Land in ourselves. We never seem to realize that. Ordinarily we tell people, "If you do something bad, you will surely be destined for some undesirable place. But if you behave yourself, you will be born in the Pure Land. How happy you will be," and so on.

In Japanese, and perhaps in Chinese, we have a saying: Give a child a yellow leaf and he will play with it as if it were really gold. We play with yellow leaves, thinking that they are valuable. In fact, we play with yellow leaves a great deal. How guileless we are! It is really wonderful. We find inner self when *Namu Amida Butsu* is pronounced once for all. My conclusion is that Amida *is* our inmost self, and when that inmost

The Enlightenment of the Inner Self

self is found we are born in the Pure Land. The kind of Pure Land located elsewhere, where we stay, is most undesirable. What is the use of lingering in the Pure Land, enjoying ourselves and doing nothing? Most people dont' think about that, and it's a good thing. If they thought about it, they would become so dissatisfied with themselves and put themselves into trouble. It is better not to think of those things.

God seems cruel to put us human beings into this hot place and make us suffer so much. But nothing awakens us to religious consciousnes like suffffering.

three
THE REALITY OF FAITH

Human beings find names essential. Names are discriminating; they distinguish one thing from another. By distinguishing one object from another object, we are aided in understanding. If we did not know the nature of an object to which we have given a certain name, it could not be distinguished from another object. Therefore discrimination is essential to understanding objects. But names are not everything.

Another unique aspect of human beings is this: Men by nature manufacture all kinds of tools. Names are also tools. With names we handle objects. But inventing tools may lead to the "tyranny of tools." When tools become tyrannous, instead of our making use of them, they rebel against their inventors and take revenge. Then we are made tools of the tools we make. This strange process is especially noticeable in modern life. We invent many machines, which in turn control our human affairs, human life. Machines, especially in recent years, have inextricably entered our life. We try to adjust ourselves to the machine, because the machine refuses to obey our will once it's out of our hands.

In our intellectual processes, ideas are also despotic, and we cannot always control concepts. We invent or construct many ideas, many concepts. They are very useful to us in handling our life, but convenient ideas frequently become despotic and, indeed, control their inventors. Scholars, who invent ideas, forget they formulated those concepts in order to handle realities for a specific purpose. Each science, whether it is called biology or psychology or astronomy, has its own premises, its own hypotheses. Each science organizes the field it has chosen—stars, animals, fish, and so on—and handles

The Reality of Faith

those realities according to the concepts it has especially invented to enable it to discuss those objects with understanding. Scientists, in pursuing their theories, in exercising their ideas, sometimes find themselves in situations not explainable by those concepts. Then, instead of dropping those ideas and trying to create new concepts so that the unexpected difficulties could be included and well handled, they stick to the first ideas they have made and try to make new realities obey old concepts. Or they simply exclude those things which are not caught up in the networks of ideas they have invented.

You might say some scientists catch fish in a net with certain standardized meshes. Those fish which cannot be scooped up and contained in their net will be dropped out—they won't be considered worth saving. The scientist-fishermen just take up those that can be caught in the net and try to explain their catch by means of the ideas they have already made. Other fish are supposed not to exist. The person holding the net says, "These exist, these that have been caught up in my net. All other fish are nonexistent."

The example can be extended to astronomy. When stars do not come into the scope of an existing telescope, those stars are neglected. The invention of a very powerful telescope would enable the astronomer to survey the sky more widely and more extensively. But when some astronomers are asked about those parts of space which cannot come into the scope of existing telescopes, they shrug as if that were unimportant. Sometimes they even go so far as to say space is empty beyond certain groups of stars. Certain galaxies make up their astronomical maps, and beyond those, they maintain, there is a void.

Such conclusions are altogether unwarrantable. If scientists were content with making conclusions on what they could survey or measure, that would be all right. If they maintain that beyond that they do not know, and they don't venture any theory or any hypothesis, that is all right too. But blinded by their own brilliance, by whatever success they have already achieved within certain boundaries, they try to extend that success beyond those boundaries, as if they had already surveyed and measured what they actually do not know. That is the trouble with most scientists.

The trouble with ordinary people is that they blindly rely on what scientists say. But scientists must always condition their statements, for they all start with certain hypotheses. Formerly, scientists couldn't explain light, so they invented what they called "wave theory." But wave theory did not account for all the phenomena connected with light, so scientists introduced that which

The Reality of Faith

they called "quantum theory." This made the explanation of other phenomena possible. Then it was discovered that to explain all the phenomena, they had to use *both* theories. Unfortunately, those hypotheses contradict each other. So when wave theory is adopted, quantum theory must be thrown out; if quantum is taken up, the other theory must be discarded. But certain phenomena exist. Scientists cannot deny the reality of those phenomena. So, however contradictory, two theories have to be adopted, and somehow they have to coexist.

Furthermore, our five senses are here, and because of them reality—our survey of reality—is connected to those five senses. If we had another sense, or two or three more senses, outside of our existing five senses, something altogether different might exist. If we say our five senses exhaust reality, that is too presumptive on our part. We can say that as far as our five senses and our intellect can comprehend, the world is to be understood, explained, and interpreted in a certain manner. But there is no way to deny the existence of something—or it may or may not be proper to say "someone"—something higher or something deeper, something more extensively covering the field. There may be something beyond the measure of our five senses and our intellect. If we do possess some such thing in ourselves, perhaps largely underdeveloped, if we have another way of coming in contact with reality that is much deeper, more extensive, than our senses and intellect permit, it is presumptuous of us to deny such an "intuition" and say, "There is no such thing—nothing exists outside my senses and intellect."

We are arrogant if we deny this higher and deeper intuition, especially the *myōgō*. *Myōgō* is not the correct word but we call it *myōgō*, though it contains something more. The efficacy of *myōgō* in allowing us into the Pure Land offers a realization of the highest reality, a full grasp of ultimate truth. *Myōgō* does not work on our senses and intellect, which are relative; it works on the part of our being which extends beyond the senses and intellect, and if I deny the efficacy of the *myōgō* to explore those fields of human beings which cannot be surveyed by intellection, those who are addicted to interdiction deny the existence of such fields.

In religious life there is a peculiar experience that we call "faith." Faith is quite a strange and wonderful thing. In ordinary life when we say "faith" or "belief," we mean something which our knowledge does not necessarily certify, something beyond our ordinary comprehension. Yet in religious faith we reach a point at which we have to venture into that life opened up by faith. In the relative faith of our natural life we can say,

The Reality of Faith

"Unless I have seen it or unles I have heard it myself personally, I cannot believe it." If we accept anything not by means of our direct personal experience but through the communication of our friends or books and so on, judging the basis on which that belief is established as adequate, we think the evidence is strong enough, verifiable enough to accept as true. We believe, even though the evidence is outside our direct personal experience. But in religious belief there is something more than that.

Even when our intellect is unable to verify what scientists would call objective or scientific truth, yet there is something in religious faith which somehow compels us to accept that belief as reality. Though we have not yet experienced it, and we probably may never experience it, still it almost demands our acceptance, whether we will or not. There is a danger—a certain decision one has to make whether to accept that faith or not. This is the way all theologians talk about accepting faith. It is a kind of venturesome deed or experience, plunging into a certain unknown region and deciding to risk one's faith or ones' destiny.

I am afraid people who have such a theology are still on the plane of relativity. The fact is that we are compelled—there is no choice but to acept that faith. All religions contain a similar idea of that nature. Instead of Amida's getting into our life or our being, our being is carried away by Amida. That is the way *myōgō* begins to live, to become actual life with Shin devotees. Some people ask about the significance of *myōgō* and how *myōgō* could be so efficacious as to take us to Amida and make us born in the land of purity. As long as a person has such doubt or suspicion or hesitancy in accepting *myōgō* in true faith, then he is not yet in it.

In India there is a mythical bird, the golden-winged bird. It is told in the sutra that it is a very big bird. It eats dragons for its food. The dragons live deep in the ocean, but when the golden-winged bird from above detects the dragons way down at the bottom of the ocean, it sweeps down from the sky, the waves open up, and it picks the dragons out of the deep and eats them. Of course the dragons are afraid of the approach of that bird and dread becoming its meal.

There is another story, of which I shall only tell part, in connection with the golden-winged bird. Somebody asked a Buddhist teacher, "A bird who has broken through the net—what does he eat?" The mythical bird, having broken through the net, is perfectly free. He is absolute master of himself. We usually find ourselves bound up with all kinds of nets, most of them made by ourselves. The nets may not really exist, but we imagine we are trapped in them. Now this bird—that is, one

The Reality of Faith

of us who has been spiritually enlightened—is the one who has broken through the nets. The bird is, by way of analogy, the spiritually free man. When the Buddhist teacher was asked, "What would be the food that this bird eats?" he meant: What kind of life would a really free, spiritually enlightened man need? One who has full belief in the *myōgō*, one who is possessed by Amida, what sort of life would he lead? What kind of man would he be?

That's the kind of question we often ask. In fact most of us or all of us ask that question, though it does not concern us at all. What's the use of trying to know such things instead of being those things ourselves? Because we are so curiously made, we always try to ask questions which do not really concern us. That is the frailty of human nature, but at the same time it points up how significantly our human life is distinct from animal life. Animals don't ask such questions.

The master said to his questioner, "*You* come through the net yourself. Then I will tell you." When one has "come through the net" he needs no telling. He knows himself. So instead of asking the idle question, "What would be the life of one who is really spiritually free?" why don't you be free yourself spiritually, and see what kind of life it is? In the same way a person asks, "What will be the life of a Shin devotee?" Or nowadays Americans often ask me, "What significance does the message of Buddhism have for our modern life?" Instead of being informed about all the advantages that accrue from the objective—for instance, in Shinshu's case, *myōgō*—we may explain all kinds of benefits, all kinds of advantages, material or otherwise, which come from the belief in *myōgō*. Rather, you should just accept *myōgō* and try to live it. Or instead of trying, just live it. Then you will know what it means.

This is what distinguishes religious life from worldly life, or relative life. In relative life we want to know beforehand all that may come after we have done this or that. Then we expect a certain outcome. But in religious life we accept and know, at the same time living that which is beyond knowledge, so in knowing and living, living becomes knowledge and knowing becomes living. This kind of difference sharply divides religious life from worldly life. In fact, there is no such thing as spiritual life distinguished from worldly life. Worldly life is spiritual life, and spiritual life is worldly life.

But we are blinded, mixed up with worldly affairs. Our scientists are caught up by a net they themselves have woven. In the same way we are blinded by our own inventions, assuming inventions are realities. We have to fight these unrealities. What we want is not exactly unreality. What we want is real enough, but with

The Reality of Faith

certain conditions, certain limitations. That is what we frequently refuse to do.

Now regarding *myōgō*, Shinran, the founder of the Shin sect, says, "Once *myōgō* is pronounced, that is enough to make you born in the Pure Land." Being born in the Pure Land is an event that takes place while we are still living in this life.

I was reading a certain Christian book recently in which the author spoke about Christ's being born in the soul. We generally think Christ was born on a certain historical date so many chronological years ago, he was born in a certain part of the earth, and he was born by the miraculous power by God, not in the usual biological way. But this Christian author says, "Christ is born in our soul, and when we recognize that birth, when we become conscious of Christ's being born within us, that is the time we are saved." So Christ is born in the course of history, but that historical event takes place in our own spiritual life. Christ is born when we must become conscious of his birth in us. He was not actually born in any specific place, but he is being born in us every day, every minute. He was not born once in history, but his birth is repeated everywhere at any moment. And his birth is dependent on this, the Christian author says: the death of all our selfish desires. We must die to ourselves. We must die to what we call evil. When evil is altogether forsaken and the soul is no longer disturbed, there will be no anxiety, no annoyance, no worries whatever, for all worries come from our being addicted to the idea of self. Therefore, when the self is surrendered, all storms are quieted and absolute peace, complete silence, prevails in the soul.

It is wonderful that this Christian writer speaks of silence. When silence prevails in the soul, that is the moment when Jesus Christ is born in our soul. So the silence is needed. When everything is kept quiet, the opportunity is opened for spiritual being to come into our soul. Silence is attained when self is given up. When self is given up, the consciousness of duality is altogether unknown.

When I say dualism no longer exists, I do not mean the annihilation of duality itself. Duality is somehow left as it is and yet its two identities are combined. So two are left as two and yet there is a state of identity between them. At this time silence takes place. When there are two, two means more than two—that is, multiplicities. When there are multiplicities there are all kinds of noise, all kinds of disturbance. The noise is silenced—but this silence is not accomplished by the annihilation of those multiplicities. The multiplicities are left as they are, yet silence prevails, not underneath, not inside, not outside, but there. Christ's birth takes

The Reality of Faith

place in this kind of silence. The realization of silence is simultaneously the birth of Christ. They occur synchronously.

Myōgō comes to our active life when there is no more *myōgō* besides Amida. Amida becomes *myōgō*, and *myōgō* becomes Amida. That is the time that I spoke about, the joining of *hō* and *ki*. When *myōgō* is pronounced and we are conscious of saying *Namu* to Amida, and when Amida, listening to us, says *Namu*, there will be no identity, no silence. One is calling out to the other, the other looking down or looking up. This means dualism and not silence or disturbance.

But when *Namu* is Amida, Amida is *Namu*. *Ki* is *hō*. *Hō* is *ki*. This is silence. When this silence takes place, when *myōgō* is absolutely identified with Amida, then *myōgō* ceases to be the name of somebody who exists outside the one who calls that *myōgō* up. This is the perfect identity or absolute identity—but it is not to be called oneness. When we say "one" we interpret that "one" numerically, that is, as standing against two, three, four, and so on. But in this oneness, absolute oneness cannot be measured, for it goes beyond our measurement. In this kind of oneness, absolute oneness, absolute identity, *myōgō* is Amida, Amida is *myōgō*. There is no separation between the two, and *ki* and *hō* are identical.

This absolute faith is reality. This is the moment, as indicated by Shinran, that if you say *Namu Amida Butsu* once, it is enough to save you. That the "one" is "absolute one" is quite mysterious.

four

THE FUTILITY OF PRIDE

"In order for the devotee to be saved by Amida and welcomed to the Pure Land when he pronounces the *myōgō—Namu Amida Butsu,* in all sincerity—the devotee cannot know what is good or bad for him. All is left to Amida. This is what I, Shinran, have learned." What Shinran says—that all is left to Amida—goes directly against our moral consciousness, what we call conscience. But from the religious point of view, what we think is good is not necessarily good all the time or absolutely good. At any time, good can turn into bad, and vice versa. So we cannot be the absolute judge of moral good or moral evil. When, by Amida's help, we go beyond the gap, then everything is left to Amida's workings. When we become conscious of his workings in everything we do, we do not know what is good or what is bad, yet whatever we do is all good. This is a paradox, and as long as we live on this plane it is inexplicable. It goes beyond our comprehension.

"Amida's vow," Shinran continues, "is meant to make us all attain supreme Buddhahood." As I said before, when supreme enlightenment is attained we realize the presence of the Pure Land, that we are right in the midst of the Pure Land. We realize the supreme Buddhahood, which is the same as supreme enlightenment, when we find that we are in the Pure Land itself.

"Now," Shinran goes on, "Buddha is formless, and because of his formlessness he is known all by himself." All physical things have form, and ideas have something to designate, but when Buddhists say "formlessness," they mean neither physical form nor intellectualization; rather, they refer to a formlessness which goes beyond the materiality of things and our habits of intellectual-

The Futility of Pride

izing. Formlessness in this sense is uniquely a Buddhist term. And this formlessness, *jinen*, means "all by himselfness," or "being by itselfness." If Amida had a form, he would not be called the Supreme Tathagata, Nyorai. As an indication of his formlessness, he is called Amida. This is what Shinran learned.

When we have understood this, we need not be concerned with *jinen* any longer. This is important. When we realize that we are really living in the world of formlessness, we have no more need of talking about *jinen*, "being by itself."

Shinran goes on, "When you turn your attention to it, the meaningless meaning assumes a meaning which defeats its own purpose." When we talk about "being by itself," we no longer are "being by itself." There is no more "meaningless meaning." Meaning now means something. It points out something else. When we are "meaning itself," we need not talk about meaning anymore. When we are *jinen* itself, there is no more discussion of it, because we are *jinen*. All kinds of troubles arise in our reasoning about things. When we begin to think, we find numerous difficulties, but when we don't think, everything is all right. But we must not be like animals. We must remain human and yet be like the "lilies of the field" or the "fowls of the air."

Shinran says all this comes from Buddha *jnana*, Buddha-intellect or Buddha-wisdom. *Jinana* is *buttchi* in Japanese. Buddha *jnana* is *buttchi*. *Buttchi*, the "other-power," is something that goes beyond our relative way of thinking. "Other-power" is a dynamic expression. When we say *buttchi*, it is more dialectic or metaphysical. From the commentary of Shinran on *jinen hōni*, that is, "being by itself," we can see what understanding Shinran had of the working of Amida's vow-power, or the other-power.

"Meaningless meaning" may be considered as literally having no sense, without any definite content whereby we can concretely grasp its significance. Ordinarily speaking, meaningless meaning is that. In this context, meaningless meaning becomes really meaningless and has no significance to our way of living, but the idea is this: There was no teleological or eschatalogical concept on the part of Amida when he made those forty-eight vows. All the ideas expressed in them were the spontaneous outflow of his great infinite compassion, his great compassionate heart embracing everything and extending to the farthest ends of the world. This infinite compassion is Amida himself. Amida has no ulterior motive. He simply feels sorry for us suffering beings and wishes to save us from going through an endless cycle of birth and death. Amida's vows are the spontaneous expression of his love or compassion.

The Futility of Pride

It may sound strange to hear that one can go beyond teleology or purposelessness. Everything we do has a purpose in this world, but in religious life we become conscious of obtaining purposelessness, going beyond teleology, meaningless meaning, meaninglessness. And this is another mark of faith: saying, "Let thy will be done," going beyond self-power and letting Amida do his work through us or in us. Therefore there are no prayers whatever in Buddhism in the strict sense of the word "prayer," and when we pray to acquire something we will never get anything. When we pray for nothing we gain everything.

During the Tokugawa era there was a man in Japan called Issa, who was noted for his haiku. Haiku is the shortest form of Japanese poem, consisting of seventeen syllables. Issa expressed in this verse form his idea of "Let thy will be done." But in his case it has no religious implications. In fact, he was greatly involved in worldy affairs, and out of his frustration at not knowing what to do and how to do it, he uttered this haiku at the end of the year. I still remember that when I was young we paid everything we owed to the tradespeople at the end of the year. In my day it was twice a year, once in July and the rest at the end of the year. If we could not pay everything by the middle of July we left it until the end of the year, and if we could not pay then, we went broke. Issa was in such trouble. I will give his haiku first in Japanese, for those who understand Japanese will appreciate it:

> *Nani goto mo*
> *Anata makase no*
> *Toshi no kure.*

This means Issa was in a terrible impasse: "I, being at the end of the year, having no money whatever to pay all my accounts, have no alternative but to let Amida do his will." If Amida could take care of all of Issa's poverty, there would be nothing better in this world, for Issa was really poor. He was poverty-stricken in more than earthly goods. Worldly poverty and spiritual poverty—sometimes they go hand in hand.

In reading Meister Eckhart, I found a story you might like to hear: A daughter came to the preaching cloister and asked for Meister Eckhart. The doorman asked, "Whom shall I announce?"

"I don't know," she said.

"Why don't you know?"

"Because I am neither a girl, nor a woman, nor a husband, nor a wife, nor a widow, nor a virgin, nor a master, nor a maid, nor a servant."

The doorman went to Meister Eckhart and said, "Come out here and see the strangest creature you

The Futility of Pride

ever heard of. Let me go with you as you stick your head out and ask, 'Who wants me?'"

Meister Eckart did so, and she gave him the same reply she had made to the doorman.

Then Meister Eckhart said, "My dear child, what you say is right and sensible, but explain to me what you mean."

She said, "If I were a girl I should still be in my first innocence. If I were a woman I should always be giving birth in my soul to the eternal world. If I were a husband I should put up a stiff resistance to all evil. If I were a wife I should keep faith with my dear one whom I married. If I were a widow I should be reverently devout. If I were a servant maid, in humility I should count myself lower than God or any creature. If I were a manservant I should be hard at work, always serving my lord with my humble whole heart. But since of all of these, I am not one, I am just a something among some things, and so I go."

Then Meister Eckhart went in and said to his pupils, "It seems to me that I have just listened to the purest person I have ever known."

This story is entitled "Meister Eckhart's Daughter." I have something to add here: This strange daughter said, "Of all of these, I am not one." She considered herself uncharacteristic of all those enumerated. They were doing nothing in a worldly sense, but she mixed this up with a spiritual sense. "If I were a husband," she said, "I should put up a stiff resistance to all evil." That statement is made in a worldly sense—but also in a somewhat spiritual sense, I believe. If one is engaged in a spiritual life, there is some end to perform. If you believe in this or that end, if you have some work to accomplish, you will have something. But she says, "Since of all of these, I am not one, I am just a *something* among some things." I wouldn't say this. I would say, "I am just a *nothing* among some things, and so I go." "So I go" is *jinen hōni*. It is *sono-mama*. It is "Let thy will be done." This is quite an interesting story, I think.

Now let us return to our discussion of other-power *Jiriki* is self-power. *Tariki* is other-power. The Pure Land school is known as the other-power school because it teaches that *tariki* is most important in attaining rebirth in the Pure Land or regeneration or enlightenment or salvation. Whatever name we may give to the end of our religious efforts, that end comes from the other-power, not from self-power. This is the contention of Shin followers.

Other-power is opposed to what is known in theology as syngerism, which means that in the work of salvation man has to do his share just as much as God does his.

The Futility of Pride

This is Christian terminology. The Shin school may therefore be called monadism, in contrast to synergism. *Syn* means together, and *ergism* means work—"working together." Monadism means working alone. *Tariki* means working alone, without self-power. The other-power school is monadism instead of synergism. It is all Amida's work. The relative existences which we ordinary people lead have nothing to do with effecting our birth in the Pure Land. Our rebirth in the Pure Land, in other words, will be attaining Enlightenment.

Monadism may be illustrated by the behavior of cats. When the mother cat carries her kittens, she grasps the neck of each kitten with her mouth and carries it from one place to another. That is monadism because the kittens just let their mother carry them. Monkeys, however, are carried on their mother's back. Baby monkeys grasp their mother's body with their limbs or tails, so the mother is not doing the work alone. The baby monkeys do their part. The cat's way is monadism, for the mother alone does the work. The monkey's way is synergism, for two work together.

In Shinshu teaching, Amida is almost the only important power that works—we just let Amida do his work. We don't add anything of our own to Amida's working. This doctrine, other-power, or monadism, is based on the idea that we humans are relative-minded, and as long as we are so constituted there is nothing in us, no power which will enable us to cross the stream of birth and death. Amida must come from the other side and carry us on the boat of all efficient vows—that is, by means of his *hongan*, his friendly Dharma.

There is a deep and impassable chasm between Amida and ourselves, and we are so heavy-laden with Karma hindrance that we cannot shake it off by our own power. Amida must come and help us, extend his arms of help from the farther end. This is what generally is taught by the Shin school. But from another point of view, however ignorant and impotent and helpless we may be, we will never grasp Amida's arms unless we exhaust everything we have in our efforts to reach the other end.

It is all right to say other-power does everything by itself. We just let it accomplish its work, but we must nevertheless become conscious of the other-power's doing its work in us. Unless we are conscious of Amida's doing his work, we shall never be saved. We can never be conscious or sure of the fact that we are born in the Pure Land and have attained our Enlightenment. To acquire this consciousness, we must exhaust all our efforts. Amida may be standing and beckoning us to come to the other shore where he is standing, but we cannot see Amida until we have done all we can do.

The Futility of Pride

Self-power is not what is needed, really, to cross the stream. Amida will extend his arms of help only when we realize that our self-power is of no account.

Since we cannot achieve the end we try to accomplish, Amida's help must be recognized. We must become conscious of it. In fact, recognition comes only after we have strained all our efforts to cross the stream by ourselves. We only realize the inefficacy of self-power when we try to make use of that power, when we become conscious of how worthless self-power is. The other-power is all-important, but this all-importantness is known only to those who have striven, by means of self-power, to attempt the impossible.

This realization or the worthlessness of self-power may also be Amida's work. In fact it is, but until we achieve recognition we do not realize that Amida has been doing all this for us and in us. Therefore, striving is a prerequisite of realization. Spiritually or metaphysically speaking, everything is finally from Amida, but we must remember that we are relative beings. As such, we cannot survey things unless we first try to do our best on this plane of relativity. Crossing from the relative plane to the transcendental or absolute plane—the plane of the other-power—may be impossible, logically speaking, but it appears an impossibility only before we have tried everything on this side. So the relativity of our existence, the complete striving or exhausting of ourselves, self-power—these are all synonyms. The idea is known in Japanese as *hakarai*.

Hakarai, quite a technical term with Shin people, is similar to the Christian idea of pride. Christians, who in a way are not so philosophical as Buddhists, do not use terms such as self-power or other-power. Only theologians use that kind of terminology. Ordinarily, Christians use the word "pride," which exactly corresponds to the Shin idea of *jiriki*, self-power. This pride is self-assertion, complimenting oneself as being worthy, someone who can accomplish great things. To rely on self-power is pride, and such pride is very difficult to uproot, as is belief in self-power.

In this world of relativity our every action depends on self-power. On the moral plane, especially, we talk constantly about individual responsibilities, making one's own choice, and coming to a decision—all products of self-power. As long as we live in a moral world, individual responsibility is essential. If we acted without any sense of responsibility, society would really be chaotic and end in suicide. Therefore self-power or pride is needed in this normal world of relativity, especially when life proceeds smoothly, that is, without encountering any hindrance or anything that frustrates our ambitions, imaginations, or ideals. But as soon as we

The Futility of Pride

encounter something which stands athwart the way we want to go, then we are forced to reflect upon ourselves.

Such obstructions in life may be enormous, inot only individually but collectively. As our society gets more and more complex, the hindrances or obstructions increasingly become more collective in nature, and individuals feel decreasingly responsible for them. But when a society—or a community or a congregation or a gathering of individuals—is involved, whether the individuals are conscious of it or not, each one has to be responsible to a greater or lesser degree for what his society does, what society imposes on its members. When we encounter such hindrances, we reflect upon ourselves and find we are altogether impotent to overcome them. If we did not have any obstacles on our way, things might proceed smoothly, safely. But the very moment we encounter an obstacle that seems insurmountable, we reflect and find our self-power completely inadequate to cope with massive difficulties.

Then we feel frustrated, and all kinds of anxiety, uncertainty, fear, and worry begin to multiply. Such feelings, in fact, characterize modern life. This is where pride fails to provide an answer. Pride is curbed at this point. It has to give way to something higher or stronger. Then pride is humiliated. In our relative world, on this plane of conditionality, such obstacles are bound to appear as long as we live. They cannot be avoided.

Earlier Buddhists used to say, "Life is suffering, life is pain, and we are compelled to try to escape from it or transcend the necessity of being shackled to birth and death." They used the words "emancipation," "liberation," and "escape." Nowadays, instead of such terminology, we say, "to attain freedom," "to transcend," or "to synthesize."

Now we have transcended relativity, striving, self-power, *hakarai*, and pride, making no efforts. This relative world is characterized by all kinds of strivings, and unless we strive we cannot get anything. But in religious life there are no efforts, no strivings. Self-power is replaced by other-power, and pride by humility. *Hakarai* is what is known as *jinen hōni*, a very important term. The Japanese say *Anata makase*. *Anata* means "you," or "other," or "thou." *Makase* means "Let thy will be done," a Christian phrase. *Jinen hōni* means roughly "Into the other-power." It might also be translated "Let thy will be done."

Shinran, the founder of the Shin sect, spoke about *jinen hōni—Anata makase*, or "Let thy will be done." His interpretation is somewhat scholastic, but I will present it for your thinking. *Ji* of *jinen* means "of itself"

The Futility of Pride

or "by itself." *Ji* literally means "thing as it is," for it is not due to the designing of man but Amida's vow that man is born in the Pure Land. Man is naturally, or spontaneously—this is the meaning of *nen*—led to the Pure Land. The devotee does not make any conscious self-designing efforts, for self-power is altogether ineffective to achieve the end of being born in the Pure Land or attaining enlightenment. *Jinen* thus means that because one's rebirth in the Pure Land is wholly due to the working of Amida's vow-power, the devotee simply believes in Amida and lets his vow work itself out.

When I say "rebirth in the Pure Land," it is to be understood in a modern way; that is, going to the Pure Land is not an event which takes place after death. The Pure Land is experienced while here, and we are carrying it with us all the time. In fact, Pure Land is surrounding us everywhere. We become conscious of it, we recognize that Amida has come to help us, after strivings have been experienced and exhausted. Then *jinen hōni* comes along. *Hōni* means "It is so because it is so."

We cannot give any reason for our living here. Why do we live here? The answer necessarily is: We live because we live. Explanations for our existence inevitably result in a contradiction, and we cannot live with such a contradiction, even for a moment. But contra-

SHIN BUDDHISM

tradition does not get the better of us—we get the better of it.

In this connection, with the *tariki* and *jiriki* idea, other-power and self-power, it means this: It is in the nature of Amida's vow-power that we are born in the Pure Land. Therefore the way in which other-power works may be defined as "meaning with no meaning." This is a contradiction or a paradox. When we talk about "meaning," we wish the word to signify something, but in religious experiences, "meaning" has no meaning whatever. That is to say, its workings are so natural, so spontaneous, so effortless, so absolutely free, that it works as if it were not working.

The idea of reincarnation is justified. If we did not reincarnate ourselves we could never sympathize with all beings. Today there is a great deal of experimentation on mice and pigs and dogs. Scientists inject drugs into animals to test the effects. They act as if experimental animals were mere inanimate instruments in their hands. Medical doctors who experiment with animals claim their research will result in medicinal advances or new surgical techniques for us human beings. But what sort of human beings are we? Are all human beings so desirable that their lives must be saved?

The Futility of Pride

There are many kinds of human beings. I cannot judge the validity of all life, but from some point of view, many people are continuing existences which are not highly desirable. For instance, most of us, as we live our lives here today, are not worthy at all. A certain view of life can lead to thinking of war and inventing terrible weapons to kill, slaughter, and massacre. But that is another matter.

To experiment on innocent mice and cats and dogs is indefensible. We cannot just go on unconcerned about them. "Well, they have no consciousness," we might say. "Their lives do not mean anything." But at the same time there is something in every one of us, I think, which makes us sorry for all innocent victims. Medical experimentation is not in itself evil, but there must be a certain instinct in ever one of us that makes us hesitant to cause any being to suffer without feeling some kind of—not remorse or regret—but some kind of pity, some kind of compassion. Such pity or compassion arises from our instinctual awareness of once having been those mice or dogs or pigs. Otherwise we can never feel compassion. Compassion means empathy, feeling a oneness with others.

five

THE EXCELLENCE OF MAN

Let us now consider *myōkōnin*. *Myō* means "wonderful." *Myōkōnin* connotes a "wonderfully good man," or "excellent man," and it is a word we generally use to designate the most devoted follower of Shin teaching. *Myōkōnin* is not used to describe any other Buddhist sect members. It refers exclusively to devoted Shin Buddhist followers.

These followers are distinguished generally by their goodheartedness, kindheartedness, unworldliness, piousness, and, lastly, by their illiteracy. Generally, they are not well educated and do not know much about sophisticated living or scholarship. More noteworthy yet, they are unable to understand the teachings of Shin. If they were learned or if they were more sophisticated, then their expressions would not come so directly from the heart. Since they are not highly literate, they are not spoiled by worldly living. Therefore what they feel comes out untainted by intellect. Their thought is touched by sincerity, and one senses it in going over their writings. But usually they don't write much. They act instead of writing, and their acts are sometimes quite noteworthy.

I remember one example. Most of the large Buddhist temples are located in Kyoto. In the country, about 200 miles away from Kyoto, lived a very pious man. One day he heard that a big fire was burning up the temple to which he belonged. He immediately took a large carpet, soaked it in water, and shook it toward the door of the temple in which the fire was supposed to be taking place. Now a small fire can effectively be put out by smothering it with a wet blanket. If it is a big fire, the blanket itself may be consumed. But when this pious man heard of the fire, he could not help going

The Excellence of Man

out and committing himself to the stupidest of all possible actions.

When one's thought processes are intellectual, rationalization sees into the futility of such an attempt to extinguish a fire. But when there is no such medium of intellection, grief comes into one's mind and one immediately responds, "The fire must be put out," especially when it is burning an important church. When the pious man hears this news, his immediate response, without any mediation of intellect, is to go out and shake the wet blanket.

Such irrationally impulsive action is, from the worldly point of view, the height of stupidity and absurdity. At the same time, from another point of view which we might call spiritual or religious, this man's act makes us ponder most deeply. Rationally stupid? Yes! But also a certain genuineness of his feeling expresses itself in this act, and that ingenuousness, that immediacy of response without any interference between feeling and expression, most distinguishes the class of people of which I speak.

There is another story about *myōkōnin*. When a man heard noise going on in his yard, he looked out and saw the boys of the neighborhood climbing up one of the trees in his orchard, trying to steal the fruit. The man quietly went out and put up a ladder underneath the boys who were up in the tree, then he quietly returned to his house. Is that not a stupid action? Boys are stealing his property, and the owner does not stop them from completing their unlawful act. This devotee, this *myōkōnin*, fears that when the children try to come down stealthily out of the tree, so the master won't know they are stealing his fruit, they might slip, fall down to the ground, and get hurt. His impulse is to prevent them from being harmed, not to save his property from unlawful thieves. Such action is characteristic of *myōkōnin*.

Another story of *myōkōnin* is literary. This is quite an unusual case. As I have said, *myōkōnin* do not usually commit themselves to writing, for writing generally goes through the intellect, and when the intellect interposes itself, expression becomes warped and insincere. This man, whose name was Saichi, died about twenty years ago, when he was a few years over eighty. His profession was making *geta*, a primitive sort of footgear. Even today many Japanese wear *geta*, a type of wooden shoe. Saichi made use of his wood shavings. Whatever came into his mind, he wrote down on these shavings. In the evening he would gather them up and transfer his words into the type of notebook used by schoolchildren in those days. Thus he kept up a kind of religious journal, you might say, for more than twenty years. Saichi

The Excellence of Man

was confirmed in the Shin faith when he was around fifty years old. He began searching after Shin truth when he was nineteen and spent about thirty years getting to the truth of Shin teaching.

So attaining the truth is no easy task. It is no joke, not just talk to pass the time. It is really serious work. Shin especially is more difficult really to understand than other teachings of Buddhism. Shin teachers say than Shin is the easiest way to attain Buddahood, but to my mind, it is the most difficult way to attain Buddahood.

Before I return to Saichi, let me quote one of the still-living *myōkōnin*. She is a truly illiterate woman whom I met when I was in Japan a few years ago. Because she does not know how to write, she told this to her son, who was about to go away from her. She dictated what I am going to tell you, and told her son to put it into writing. When I saw her she was about sixty.

When this woman first married she was somewhat unhappy, I think, according to her story, and she used to go to a Buddhist temple nearby and listen to the sermons. When she went out to the temple, she tried to keep her mother-in-law from knowing about it. So there must have been certain disagreement between her and her mother-in-law, not between her and her husband.

SHIN BUDDHISM

But in Japan a woman marries not only a husband but the whole family. Even today, to a certain extent, the old lady of the house is quite despotic. About fifty years ago, this was especially true. This young woman had great trouble for many years until one day she realized the truth of Shin teaching. When her son had to leave her to become an apprentice in a larger city, she was grieved at parting with him. There was nothing for her to do but try to make her son understand and receive what she already had. She wanted him to comprehend the faith in Shin teaching which she had accepted. Therefore she dictated to him what she could not write herself.

Translations, unfortunately, do not carry the original strength and certain nice shades of meaning. English is more intellectual than Japanese or Chinese. When Japanese read their own writings, what they understand from those words is not exactly, definitively, expressed. For instance, in English I read some time ago that one of the great Christian mystics said, "God Isness is my Isness." This is quite a highly abstract expression. When God was asked what his name was, according to the Bible, he said to Moses, "My name is, I am that I am"—a quite abstract expression. In Japanese or Chinese such a highly intellectual abstract term would not be used. Also, in Japanese we have pronouns corresponding to

The Excellence of Man

your "I," "you," "he," and "she," but in many cases the subject "I," is omitted or "you" is omitted. Sometimes the object is also omitted, and only that middle term—the verb that connects subject and object and makes a sentence—alone expresses it. And how do we know that this verb expressed belongs to the subject or the object? How do we know what relationship that verb establishes between the two? All such expressions are quite vague, not stated at all. But Japanese quite liberally use what we call honorifics. By the honorific particles used we know at once "you" is meant or "I" is meant. Honorifics are not only attached to nouns but also to verbs.

So what is expressed is quite imprecise and what we hear is also quite vague, not so specifically defined as it might be in English. But this very vagueness may help in spiritual writings. Such writings belong to the spiritual life and are not so precisely definable as scientific terms, for instance. Actually this vagueness is not really vague. From the intellectual point of view it appears ambiguous because it is not well defined—subject is not specifically subject, object is not obviously object. But, spiritually speaking, subject is object, object is subject. This very indefinability, this very vague identification, is in a sense more expressive. Sometimes I think Chinese is the language most appropriate to spiritual life.

Now this is what the woman dictated to her son: "When I think of it, my heart is quickened because of my overflowing joy. Because I am illiterate, I dictate and my son writes it down, filled with as much joy as myself." Now she talks about herself. "Since childhood I was in the practice of going to the Buddhist temple, but I just listened to the sermons without paying much attention to their content. Later, however, impelled by my inner anguish, I started visiting the temple anew." Certain inner anxiety is needed. This is a necessary precursor to make one understand religious truth. Without any inner anguish, simply listening to sermons, merely reading religious writings and trying to get something out of them, is futile. Whatever we get is only a superficial shell. The woman continues, "I have found that the more I listen, the more grateful I feel, indeed, to my Oyasama. Not wanting my mother-in-law to know each time I visited the temple, I just quietly slipped out of the house. Nobody knew where I went. I thought it was all due to my self-power."

As I said before, Shin distinguishes between self-power and other-power. Self-power corresponds to Christian pride, and other-power comes through humility. When self-power or pride is crushed, then one feels humiliated, and humiliation leads to other-power. Other-power is Oyasama or Amida, or *Namu Amida Butsu*. So whenever self-power is mentioned, that means pride.

The Excellence of Man

So, she says, "I thought it was all due to my pride, self-power."

Nembutsu is another word for *myōgō*. *Nembutsu* is other-*myōgō*; when *myōgō* is other, it is *nembutsu*. It doesn't make any difference when *nembutsu* is uttered. Everything comes from the power of Oya. This is what distinguishes Shin from many other religious teachings. When self-power is abandoned, when pride is effaced, it is not due to man's self-power. It is due to other-power. In order to be really humble and experience this feeling of humility, we are apt to think we must get rid of pride and work at being humble. We might think this is done by other-power, but in the meantime we are using our own self-power. When we think it is all from the other-power, that very consciousness proves that it comes from self-power.

Other-power actually comes quite unawares to our mind. When we really have other-power, it takes complete possession of our consciousness and self-power goes away altogether. You might ask: What makes us recognize that power as other-power when it occupies the whole field of our consciousness? In fact we are not even conscious of other-power, for other-power prevails and nothing stands against it. Here the power of language is defied. Other-power is there and I am conscious of it, yet that other-power overlooks all my consciousness as myself. I am there just the same. I am I. The other is other, and yet there is consciousness which cannot be expressed. When expressed, it becomes an absurdity.

So other-power must be personally realized. When this woman writer says, "What I was imagining to be the other-power was no other than self-power," she showed that she really had the other-power. In wishing to shun the evil power and ever longing for the Pure Land, her very thought was no other than self-power. This is really the gist of religious experience.

We always wish to avoid the evil power; we always long for the Pure Land, the happy land where our rebirth takes place. We would like to be sure of that rebirth. As long as we are thinking of the other-power where we would like to be born, as long as we would like to get rid of our self-power, thinking that self-power is something to be avoided, we are still in the realm of self-power. No other power exists there. That is why *myōkōnin* especially ignore the distinction between good and bad. They are on the other side of moral thinking.

I say the religious life is always on the other side of moral life. That does not mean religious life is quite separate, sharply distinguished from the moral life. By denying the moral life we can reach the spiritual experience. When I say it is beyond moral life, I do not imply the negation of the moral life. Nor is the spiritual

The Excellence of Man

life altogether different from the moral life. The spiritual life is in the moral life, but moral life alone does not make us reach spiritual life. As long as we try to reach the spiritual realm by means of morality, we are employing self-power, and that self-power must be purged. But to try to get rid of self-power is also self-power. Now you may say in despair: "What shall I do?" That is a real problem, and we all have to go through what I call an impasse.

The woman goes on, "I have been designing"—*designing* is a special term used her—"all the time, saying, 'Is this the way or that?' But there was no designing after all. All was given fully and freely by Oyasama or Amida. How grateful I am now. *Namu Amida Butsu*."

"Design" is calculation, human effort, or motivation. Saying, "Is this the way? Is that the way?" and "What shall I do?"—that is designing. That is moral effort. That is seeking some kind of good motive. It is not quite accurate to say one should get rid of all these things. To think along such lines is to commit ourselves to the working of the self-power. At this point it is most difficult. But an ignorant woman understood this, so she could say, "I have been designing all the time, saying, 'Is this the way or that?' But there was no designing after all. All was given fully and freely by Oyasama or Amida. How grateful I am now."

She goes on, "It was because of my blindness and powerlessness that the dawn came upon me through the power of Oya." And this dawn, something breaking up or coming forth from the unknown region when we are desperate and in utter despair, when we do not know what to do, causes the light to flash through our minds. Then she utters, "How grateful I am now. *Namu Amida Butsu.* I was utterly blind and did not know it. How shameful to have thought I was all right. I thought the *nembutsu* I uttered was my own, but it was not. It was Amida's call. How grateful, indeed, I am. *Namu Amida Butsu.* Now that I am convinced of my being definitely destined for the evil path—this is also an important part, meaning hell, or everlasting fire—"neither the Pure Land nor the evil path is of any use to me."

As long as we are relative beings we are all definitely destined for what Buddhists call the evil path, and we can never walk out of the evil path. But although we live in the evil path, even as we are destined for the evil path, we are right in the middle of the Pure Land. When this is realized, we can answer, as this woman does: Neither the Pure Land nor hell—nor even purgatory, whatever it is—is of any use to me. She is now above the Pure Land. She is above the evil path or evil forms of existence. "To whom do I owe my present state of mind? To *Gokaisan sama*,* to the Rennyo

---
* I.e., *shinran shōnin.*

The Excellence of Man

Sama." These are the founders of the Shin sect, and Rennyo Sama is one of the foremost preachers in the history of Shin. "Being taught by these spiritual leaders, I have now come to this realization. My knowledge has come through all the good teachers who have successfully transmitted this doctrine. How praiseworthy they all are! *Namu Amida Butsu.* While worrying over my daily life, fretting about things wanted and wanting, I am all the time in company with Amida himself. How grateful I am. *Namu Amida Butsu.*"

Everyday life is of course full of worries, anxieties, and fears. We are living uneasily in the middle of all these troubles, whereas such difficulties do not affect *myōkōnin* at all. They have all the ordinary problems we have, but they are not so bound up with them as we are. Although they are not free from wants and fears, at the same time they are not bound by them—they are capable of freeing themselves. Though bound, yet they are free. That is what this woman says: "I am all the time in company with Amida himself." If she did not have anxieties, fears, and worries, she could never say, "All the time in company with Amida." This is the most important and significant part, and all religious experience, all religious teachings, point to such an experience. "Though in parental relationship with Amida, I cannot avoid being bothered with evil thoughts from time to time."

We often think saintly beings are so sublime that they are entirely devoid of the evil feelings we generally have. But that is not so. If we were to praise a saint for being absent from all worldly things, the saint would no doubt say, "What are you talking about? I am just as bad as you are. And yet," he would add, "I have something which makes me, in spite of all these evil thoughts, free from them and in company with God or Amida."

The woman's confession is very fine: "Though in parental relationship with Amida, I cannot avoid being bothered with evil thoughts from time to time. How shameful indeed! *Namu Amida Butsu*. No matter how hard I try not to have them, they crowd into my mind in ever-greater numbers. What a shame, indeed! *Namu Amida Butsu*. Looking at my evil self I realize what a deplorable thing it is. I am disgusted with this dear ego. How shameful! Truly I am an old hag, a disgusting evil!" But she is ever with Oyasama, who refuses to part with her. "How grateful, indeed. *Namu Amida Butsu*." She is evil, a sinful person, she is most disgusting to herself, but Oyasama never leaves her. Oyasama refuses to part with her. "Day in and day out I am with Amida. Let the sun set whenever it pleases. How grateful I am! *Namu Amida Butsu*."

To let the sun set whenever it pleases means: When-

The Excellence of Man

ever the time comes I am ready to die. When the sun sets, when my life comes to an end, I am ready to part with it and I do not care where I go. My time is always passed with Amida, no matter how unexpectedly the sun may set. "How grateful I am! *Namu Amida Butsu.* Praise and reverence to the favor I am granted! *Namu Amida Butsu.*"

What a fine declaration of Shin faith and Buddhist faith! Intellectually speaking, if one is in company with Amida all the time and conscious of the presence of the other-power, how could his mind possibly entertain or harbor any evil thoughts or feel disgusted with itself? That is what we reason by means of intellection. In actual life ambiguity and contradiction take place all the time. In spite of such contradictions, *myōkōnin*, these really religious people, are thankful and joyful for what they have experienced.

When pride is gone there is humility, and humility is recognition of the other-power. And when humility is realized we have a wonderful feeling of joy. Humility might make one feel quite miserable. Yes, it does. But simultaneously one senses a feeling quite opposite to that of misery. There is joy and there is happiness.

Now let us return to Saichi and his journal. Saichi warns us not to give up our joyous feeling, for joyousness is the very emotion that assures or confirms our faith in Shin teaching. Joy is sometimes quite precious and precarious, so you have to guard it all the time.

I will share something from Saichi's writings. He questions himself occasionally but then adds quite frequently, "Oh, Saichi, how fortunate! No worry, no fretting, no saying the *nembutsu*."

This is significant. Shin people are supposed to say the *nembutsu* all the time. If you have your faith confirmed once, all the *nembutsus* you say afterward express your gratitude. But when you visit the Shin temple, where so many people constantly utter the *Namu Amida Butsu*, you are tempted to wonder how many devoted souls are gathered there. In fact, what they are saying might be called empty *nembutsu*, for there is no feeling in it at all.

So Saichi says, "I don't say any *nembutsu*. It is not necessary. Saved by the Buddha's mercy, how grateful I feel. As for *Namu Amida Butsu*, it is ever with me. I am ever with it. While asleep, *Namu Amida Butsu*. While awake, *Namu Amida Butsu*. While walking, resting, while sitting or lying, *Namu Amida Butsu*. While working, *Namu Amida Butsu*."

In one of the songs he sings while making shoes, he says, "Footgear is joy, Saichi's joy, *Namu Amida Butsu*." This is quite significant. In modern days production is talked about extensively, but all those articles produced,

The Futility of Pride

perhaps, by the Communists, by the use of machines, are not accompanied by the joy Saichi feels in making his footgear. The result of his work shares, participates, in his feeling of joy. The *geta*, the shoes, are the symbol of joy. Not only in making *geta* does one feel joy, but in making tables, in fashioning lamps, in building houses, in paving a street, in driving a car or bus. All is joy. Everything participates in the feeling of joy.

On the management level, people are always quarreling. I can't say who is wrong or who is right. Perhaps both are on the wrong side. But if all could have this feeling that what we make shares our feeling of joy, happiness, and gratitude, then the whole world would change into a mass or habitation of joyousness. Then all work is joy. While keeping the accounts, *Namu Amida Butsu*. From within, whatever things I am engaged in, *Namu Amida Butsu* rushes out. When feeling ashamed of my wretched self, *Namu Amida Butsu*, too, so my wretchedness turns into blessedness. When joyous over the Buddha's mercy, *Namu Amida Butsu*. When feeling ashamed, *Namu Amida Butsu*. When joyous, *Namu Amida Butsu*. Everything turns into this *myōgō*, this *Namu Amida Butsu*.

Somewhere Saichi says, "Everything is not only my mind, which is filled up with so many evil thoughts. This mind, with all its evil thoughts, is brimming with

Namu Amida Butsu," And the objective world is something quite beyond our control. This objective world, according to Saichi, is filled with *Namu Amida Butsu.* Also the empty space, as it extends to the heavens or beyond the horizon, is itself filled with *Namu Amida Butsu.* Therefore everything the *myōkōnin* touches, everything he does, everything he says, is *Namu Amida Butsu.* In this case *Namu Amida Butsu* is no longer simple adoration or "I take refuge in Amida Buddha." Such a phrase seems to have no intimate pure content, no meaning, no special signification, no idea of symbolization. It is simply *Namu Amida Butsu,* simple reality. Of course, when we say "reality," we are already verging on abstraction. Just to say *Namu Amida Butsu* itself, with no explanation, is very much better.

This is the essence of Shin teaching, as I understand it. We might say the religious life has nothing to do with our practical life. In the examples of Saichi and this woman, we discover how significant the religious life can be. It expresses itself in every deed. Christian saints would agree with this. Everything is colored by this religious experience. The world becomes permeated with gratitude and joy. That does not imply everything that makes our life bad becomes extinct. It is there. It is present and yet it is nonexistent. It is there as if it were nothing. All religious teachings converge on this single point.

About the Author

Dr. Daisetsu Teitaro Suzuki was born in Kanazawa City, Japan, on October 18, 1870. He attended Waseda University and the Tokyo Imperial University. He studied Zen Buddhism under Shaku Soen. In 1893 there was a World Religious Conference in Chicago, Illinois, which Shaku Soen attended, delivering his message translated into English by Dr. Suzuki.

At the age of twenty-five he practiced Zazen (Zen meditation) and understood the Way of Buddhahood. In 1897 he went to Chicago to study and then published *The Teaching of Buddha*. He stayed in Chicago for eleven years and in 1908, at thirty-eight, visited England and Europe. The following year Dr. Suzuki became assistant professor at Gakushuin University and Tokyo Imperial University.

In 1911 he published *Self-Power and Other-Power*, a book about the Shin sect.

In 1933, at the age of sixty-three, he received a Ph.D. from the Imperial University. From 1936 to 1964 he came to the United States and toured various universities, lecturing and publishing many books on Zen and Buddhism and Japanese culture.

In 1957 he joined the Honorary Advisory Council of the American Buddhist Academy.

On July 12, 1966, at the age of ninety-six, Dr. Suzuki died in Tokyo.

During his lifetime he published more than thirty books in English and received many honors and prizes from the Japanese and Indian governments.

Design by Gloria Adelson
Set in Linotype Electra
Composed, printed and bound by the Haddon Craftsmen, Inc.
HARPER & ROW, PUBLISHERS, INCORPORATED

69 70 71 72 73 10 9 8 7 6 5 4 3 2 1